PERFORMANCE
REVIEWS

KEN LANGDON &
CHRISTINA OSBORNE

LONDON, NEW YORK, MUNICH,
MELBOURNE & DELHI

Project Editor Nina Hathway
US Editors Gary Werner, Margaret Parrish
Senior Art Editor Jamie Hanson
DTP Designer Julian Dams
Production Controller Michelle Thomas

Managing Editor Adèle Hayward
Senior Managing Art Editor Nigel Duffield

_____

Produced for Dorling Kindersley by
COOLING BROWN
9–11 High Street, Hampton
Middlesex TW12 2SA

Creative Director Arthur Brown
Senior Editor Amanda Lebentz

First American Edition, 2001

4 6 8 10 9 7 5 3

Published in the United States by
DK Publishing, Inc.
375 Hudson Street
New York, New York 10014

A CIP record for this book is available
from the Library of Congress
ISBN-13: 978-0-7894-8007-1
ISBN-10: 0-7894-8007-7

Reproduced by Colourscan, Singapore
Printed in China by WKT Company Limited

See our complete product line at
www.dk.com

CONTENTS

MANAGING THE REVIEW

FOLLOWING UP THE REVIEW

INTRODUCTION

The ability to use performance reviews to develop and motivate employees is a core management skill. Regular, constructive feedback on performance is vital if staff are to build on their strengths, achieve their full potential, and make the maximum contribution to their organization. Performance Reviews equips you with all the skills and techniques you need to conduct successful reviews. It clearly explains the key goals and benefits of the review process, and leads you step-by-step through the preparation, management, and follow-up of the performance review. The book is packed with advice to help you encourage open discussion, interpret body language, build confidence, deal with performance problems, and more. With 101 practical tips scattered throughout and a self-assessment quiz that allows you to evaluate your performance review skills, this is an invaluable pocket reference to conducting reviews effectively.

UNDERSTANDING THE PURPOSE

Effective reviewing is at the heart of successful management. Understand how the review process works, and recognize how a well-managed system benefits employees and organizations.

DEVELOPING PEOPLE

Regular feedback develops staff and helps them to achieve their objectives. Create an environment in which people welcome continuous feedback, and use the performance review as a formal roundup of these ongoing, informal reviews.

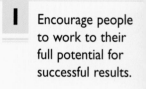

1 Encourage people to work to their full potential for successful results.

2 Praise good performance when you see it to motivate people to do even better.

PROVIDING FEEDBACK

All employees want to know how their performance is viewed by their manager. It is important to provide this feedback continuously, whether it is positive or negative. Proper feedback helps team members identify where they need to improve their skills, knowledge, and attitudes. Even highly successful achievers need feedback to help them sustain their performance. Ongoing feedback improves morale, since people know exactly where they stand, and enables managers to express concerns rather than storing them up.

FORMAL REVIEWS

Formal reviews, held on a regular basis with your team members, are a culmination of continuous informal feedback. If ongoing feedback has been effective, this formal meeting will not contain any surprises for employees, and the atmosphere should be positive and businesslike. There are two parts to the formal review: the performance review and the developmental review. The performance review enables you to gain agreement from an employee on how well he or she has done in achieving objectives, and developing skills and knowledge, during the period under review. The developmental review is aimed at pinpointing what needs to be done in the future to sustain achievement or meet new objectives. This part of the review helps you to continuously improve an employee's capabilities and prepare them to take on more responsibility. Do the two parts in one review session to emphasize the link between them.

GETTING THE MOST FROM THE REVIEW

An effective review system has many benefits. Use it to:
● Sustain motivation and commitment;
● Continuously improve performance;
● Give direction and agree on expected contributions;
● Set targets in line with organizational and team goals;
● Review development so far;
● Identify training needs;
● Celebrate successes and learn from disappointments;
● Understand career aspirations and assess potential;
● Gather ideas for change.

| Provide continuous informal feedback | → | Formally review performance | → | Formally review development |

▲ DEFINING THE REVIEW

Effective reviews rely on the provision of regular feedback. This feedback is then formalized in a two-part review of a team member's performance and development.

3 Make sure that people know how important they are to the organization.

EFFECTIVE REVIEWS

Think carefully about how you will give feedback both formally and informally. In order to build for the future, it is important to be constructive in what you say and to focus on the future in the way that you say it. Make sure that all feedback is two-way, and that discussions are honest and open. Consider how you will put your points across, since people will react to the manner in which you provide feedback. Bear in mind that criticism can be difficult to take, even when an individual is aware that it is justified.

DEFINING REVIEW TYPES

There are three distinct types of reviews, each involving a different approach to evaluating performance. Understand the purpose of top-down, peer, and 360-degree reviews, and why self-assessment must feature in them all.

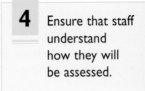

4 Ensure that staff understand how they will be assessed.

5 Find out how others in your organization view an employee's performance.

THE TOP-DOWN REVIEW

In a top-down review, the employee's immediate manager, who knows them best, is responsible for their appraisal and has the authority to set a development plan for the future. Some companies adopt a "matrix" approach in which one manager reviews an individual in terms of their contribution to a specific office or region, while another manager reviews their input to their specfic area of work. A human resources specialist, for example, with an objective of putting employees on new contracts, would be reviewed by a manager with human resources or legal expertise.

USING PEER REVIEW

In this type of review, people at the same level review their peers, so that each reviewer can use his or her expert knowledge of the employee's role and responsibilities to give an authoritative opinion on their skills. Peer review is often used for employees in professional positions, where specialized knowledge of issues such as ethics or technical competence is important. By monitoring colleagues as part of the review process, changes in practice can be fed back to the organization, and improvements made to the way members behave and work.

POINTS TO REMEMBER

● Peer review enables colleagues to act as mentors to one another, helping to improve performance all around.

● The exchange of open feedback among staff must be actively encouraged to ensure the effectiveness of peer review.

● A combination of top-down and peer review is often used to broaden the scope of feedback.

UNDERSTANDING THE 360-DEGREE REVIEW

In this type of review, the reviewer seeks feedback from everyone who has worked with the staff member, including customers, their peer group, and members of their own team. Generally, the reviewer will send out forms or questionnaires, such as customer satisfaction review forms, and then take comments into account when preparing for the formal review. There is a growing trend toward this type of review, since knowing how an employee's manager, peers, internal customers, external customers, and others view his or her performance often provides valuable insight.

6 See that questions on customer forms provide useful feedback.

7 Evaluate feedback carefully to ensure its value to the staff member.

USING SELF-ASSESSMENT

Self-assessment encourages employees to play an active role in the review process. The fact that people tend to be hard on themselves in a self-assessment can make the review more successful. As their manager, you are likely to be less harsh, and can focus on the positive aspects of their answers, praising achievements and strengths. Self-assessment questions should be framed to ensure that they help the employee to analyze their performance effectively. Answering the questions set should enable the staff member to prepare for the review itself, and to uncover any need for change.

Avoid posing questions designed to lead an employee into giving evidence to support your own preconceived opinions. This will not result in a constructive review.

ENCOURAGING ▶ REFLECTION
Self-assessment helps staff to feel included in the review process. It prompts them to consider where they are going and how they are doing.

SETTING OBJECTIVES

*R*eviews provide the opportunity to establish objectives in line with an organization's strategy. Bear in mind that up-to-date job descriptions are vital if you are to use reviews to discuss, revise, and align objectives to your organization's goals.

8 Plan ahead and make allowances for any future changes.

9 Ensure that you are prepared for the arrival of new employees.

PRIMING NEW EMPLOYEES

The process of setting objectives will begin as soon as a new member of staff joins your team. Orientation sessions should be used to introduce newcomers to the goals of your organization, and followup meetings should be held afterward to as new employees for feedback on the orientation, agree on job descriptions, and set performance objectives. If you fail to hold this meeting, a new recruit could be working for months before reviews take place. Use the meeting to pinpoint training needs, identify other members of staff to be met, and plan future development needs.

DOCUMENTING OBJECTIVES

Every team member needs an up-to-date job description so that they understand what is expected of them and what their objectives are. The process of establishing and documenting job descriptions can be done separately from the review to enable team members to see where they need guidance or training to perform well. Be aware that roles may change between reviews, since an individual's talents or interests in different aspects of their job can change its very nature. Reviews enable you to update job descriptions and ensure that a team member's focus is in line with that of the team and the organization.

POINTS TO REMEMBER

● Setting aside a little time every couple of months to check through and update job descriptions makes it easier to spot any changes.

● Job descriptions should clearly define overall work objectives, broken down into key areas of activity.

● Job descriptions should be as succint as possible – ideally fittin on to one 8½ x 11 inch page – ar should list main responsibilities rather than detail daily activities.

Orientation session is held to
introduce new staff to
organizational objectives

Followup meeting is held
to define responsibilities and
individual/team objectives

Job descriptions are agreed on
and documented to provide
focus and direction

Job descriptions are reviewed
regularly to maintain team
and organizational focus

Reviews are used to discuss and
refocus individuals if their job
emphasis has changed

Job descriptions are updated
if necessary, and new
objectives agreed on

11 Try to turn
intentions into
actions.

PLANNING FOR DEVELOPMENT

Just as there is a strong link between the objectives of teams in an organization, so there is a connected set of training plans. By reviewing training and development needs at each review, you will be able to match an individual's requirements to those of their team and the organization. The review and each development plan are important sources of information for organizations to plan training requirements. Personal development plans (PDPs) should specify the results you want to achieve, so that people develop in a way that helps them to achieve their objectives.

10 Use reviews as an opportunity to ensure that people are realistic about their potential.

ESTABLISHING LONG-TERM GOALS

In addition to focusing on today's results, reviews will help you to plan for the long term. By considering the potential of each team member, and discussing their career aspirations with them, you will be able to create a picture of your team in the future and produce a succession plan. Use the review to identify when it is time for an individual to move on. Consider what you will do if someone is suddenly promoted off your team, or there is a change to your role. By planning ahead, you avoid the risk of failing to deliver results during a period of transition. You also ensure that other team members are not disrupted by change and are able to maintain consistent performance.

ACHIEVING OBJECTIVES

*I*n addition to setting objectives for every
employee, reviews help to focus people on
achieving them. By agreeing on challenging,
realistic, and quantifiable performance
measures, you and your team members will
be clear on how progress will be assessed.

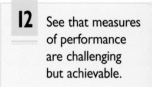
**See that measures
of performance
are challenging
but achievable.**

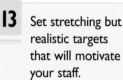
**Set stretching but
realistic targets
that will motivate
your staff.**

**Use objectives as a
way of getting the
team to focus and
work together.**

SETTING PERFORMANCE MEASURES

A key aspect of the review is to communicate
objectives with measurable criteria. Performance
that is measurable in numeric or percentage terms
will provide employees with specific targets, and
give them a sense of achievement when they
surpass them. Encourage staff to come up with
their own ideas as to what they should accept as
a challenge. They will be more committed if they
declare what is feasible themselves. Bear in mind
that employees will often set themselves bigger
challenges than those presented by a manager.
People will rarely suggest a target that is well
below what they believe they can achieve.

MAKING OBJECTIVES SMART

In a good review environment,
objectives are tested to ensure that they
are specific, measurable, agreed upon,
relevant, and timebound (SMART).
Make your objectives SMART by
ensuring that they:

● Clearly explain what the individual is
  meant to achieve – setting out exactly
  what must be done, how, and by when;

● Are measurable in terms of efficiency
  (resources used) and effectiveness
  (quality of result);

● Are proposed by the employee and
  agreed by manager after discussion;

● Are well within the employee's
  capabilities and control;

● Have a clear, unequivocal, and agreed
  upon timescale for completion.

SELECTING APPROPRIATE CRITERIA

Some performance measures cannot easily be translated into quantitative targets. Outcomes can be expressed in a number of ways, which means that it is important to select criteria that are appropriate to the individual and the particular objective. For example, in setting a performance measure for the writing of a report, an appropriate qualitative measure might be that the recipient would be able to make a confident decision after reading it. A qualitative objective, such as fast response to customer questions, may become a quantitative one if you decide to measure how many times the telephone rings before it is answered. An alternative qualitative measure could derive from a customer questionnaire that seeks feedback from customers as to whether they are satisfied with the standard of service they receive. In order to help you and the staff member find the correct measure, ask yourselves the question, "What will success look like or feel like?"

QUESTIONS TO ASK YOURSELF

Q Do I understand what our customers expect from the employee?

Q When we agree on a qualitative measure of performance, will we easily see later whether or not it has been met?

Q Is there any way we could turn a qualitative measure into a quantitative one?

Q Are we agreeing on new measures that expect performance to improve in the future?

15 Be prepared to be flexible, if necessary, should a situation change.

AGREEING ON ▶ MEASURES

Although Sally was set the objective of improving the standard of her report writing, she was unable to raise her level of performance because Tom had failed to provide her with sufficient information. By agreeing on clear measures and expectations, he provided Sally with qualitative and quantitative measures to aim for, and her performance improved dramatically.

CASE STUDY

Tom, a marketing manager, was concerned that reports written by his assistant, Sally, were poorly structured and inaccurate. He often found himself correcting her drafts several times. During her review, it was agreed that Sally should work to improve her report writing. However, after several weeks, Sally's work was still not up to the standard Tom required. He realized that in failing to set performance measures, he had not given Sally the guidance she needed to achieve her objective. He sat down with Sally and together they agreed that in the future Sally's reports should follow a set template, starting with a 500–600 word introduction and ending with a summary of the main points. They also agreed that Sally would check all facts so that Tom wouldn't need to make revisions to her drafts. As a result, Sally began to produce highly professional reports.

EMPOWERING STAFF

Team members must be committed to objectives if they are to carry out their tasks successfully. Use reviews to empower staff through delegation, to gain their commitment to actions, and to encourage them to use their own initiative.

 16 Work on the basis that everyone will want to do a good job.

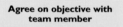
DELEGATING CONTROL OF OBJECTIVES

Agree on objective with team member

⬇

Allow team member to plan activities

⬇

Agree on team member's plan

⬇

Ask team member to suggest options if plan needs to change

⬇

Agree on performance measures with team member

17 Ask team members for their views on the way ahead.

EMPOWERING PEOPLE

By delegating responsibility to team members, you increase their control over what is achieved. This is because effective delegation involves the manager and team member agreeing on a specific and unambiguous statement of the objective and responsibility. The team member is then able to work on their own to achieve the objective, using their initiative to solve any problems along the way. Build an empowered environment by encouraging your team members to be less dependent on you as their manager. This will increase their effectiveness and save you time. Stress that you would prefer people to come to you with solutions rather than problems, particularly during the performance review. Encourage them to analyze difficult situations, to consider ways of resolving them, and to recommend appropriate actions.

DOS AND DON'TS

✔ Do allow people to learn from their own mistakes.

✔ Do encourage people to think of different options for solving a problem.

✘ Don't assume you will always have the best answer to a situation.

✘ Don't allow people's mistakes to cause them to fail in a significant objective.

CLARIFYING
RESPONSIBILITIES ▼
*During the review, encourage the team
member to take notes of what needs to be
done. They will then be able to refer to
their notes to help them summarize their
action plan at the end of the meeting.*

MAXIMIZING OWNERSHIP

Once the achievement of an objective has been delegated, the team member must fully accept its value and be committed to seeing their action plan through to success. When agreeing on objectives and plans at the review, you must both be clear what the outcome of actions should be. Without any real commitment, you run the risk that the team member will delegate the task back to you, perhaps just before the deadline. If someone is reluctant to take on responsibility, you will need to find out why they have reservations. If an employee doubts their capabilities, consider how to modify the objective so that they feel able to achieve it, or organize training or guidance to build their competence and enable them to do the job confidently.

ENCOURAGING INITIATIVE

Use the review to establish how you would like the employee to approach their work. You will not be getting involved in discussions on how they are going to go about achieving their objectives, but you should be concentrating on what needs to be achieved. You should let the employee know that you have faith in their ability and make it clear that you will be expecting them to use their own initiative. You will be setting agreed milestones to review progress so that you avoid continually asking for updates. Remember that it is important to give praise when staff make appreciable progress. "Thank you" and "Well done" are two of the most motivational phrases in the workplace.

POINTS TO REMEMBER

- People who feel able to achieve an objective in their own way will take more responsibility for that achievement.

- Good team leaders praise their people for finding new ways of getting results.

- The decision to do something is not complete until the first action is taken.

- People will take a more active part in the process of delegation if they are encouraged to question briefs and ask for more delegated responsibility.

REWARDING SUCCESS

Effective performance reviews enable you to reward achievement and encourage continuous improvement. Plan to use reviews to discuss rewards that satisfy the needs of the individual and the organization, rather than focusing on pay reviews alone.

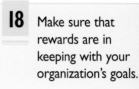

18 Make sure that rewards are in keeping with your organization's goals.

19 Always deliver rewards that have been earned by team members.

PRESENTING PRIZES ▼

Awarding prizes or vacation time is a good way of celebrating and recognizing achievement. Find out from team members during their reviews how they would like to be rewarded for good performance to give you more ideas for nonfinancial rewards.

BREAKING THE PAY LINK

There is a link between what an employee is paid and their value to the organization. You may need to make judgments about the effect of a person's performance on the pay rewards they receive. To encourage excellent performance, find other ways to reward high achievers. These people are motivated by feedback and may well become de-motivated if they see low achievers receiving the same rewards. However, if the review is seen as a hurdle that must be jumped in order to win pay increase, an employee is likely to become defensive. For this reason, appraisals are sometimes timed separately from pay reviews.

Team member receives prize as a reward for meeting objectives

Colleagues feel motivated to follow good example

ANALYZING NEEDS ▼

This simplified model of psychologist Abraham Maslow's hierarchy of needs illustrates the importance of satisfying needs at the lower levels before motivating people at higher levels. A car, a social need, may be motivational, but it will not be so until physiological needs have been met.

Self-actualization needs (development of own potential, finding self-fulfillment)

Self-esteem needs (approval from others, recognition, achievement)

Social needs (acceptance from others, affiliation, belonging)

Safety needs (feeling of security, not fearing danger)

Physiological needs (basic requirements of life, such as food and water)

MOTIVATING PEOPLE

Reviews give you an opportunity to reward your team by thanking and motivating them. The fact that you are spending time alone with them and discussing their work is in itself encouraging.

People like to know that their work is being observed by their manager. Most are also motivated by a sense of autonomy, where they feel responsible for achieving a result rather than just carrying out tasks. This helps them to feel more in control of their jobs. To keep your team motivated, delegate whenever possible. If a team member achieves success in a delegated task, their sense of achievement is a great morale booster. Finally, think about what will motivate each individual, since everyone has different needs.

BUILDING ON SUCCESS

Use reviews to develop your team by discussing past successes and achievements so that they can be repeated and even surpassed. Consider building on achievements by promoting a team member, or giving someone the chance to take part in development activities. In addition to rewarding the employee, this will also enhance their value to your organization and their ability to meet objectives. Look back at the period since the last review and discuss how the employee has used the activities in their previous development plan to improve their capabilities. This discussion helps the individual to understand the value of the development activities they have undertaken and shows them how they are improving their ability to contribute to the team and organization.

20 Find out what it is that motivates each member of your staff.

21 Remember that success often breeds further success.

PREPARING FOR THE REVIEW

Preparation is a vital part of conducting effective performance reviews. Plan all aspects of the discussion thoroughly so that staff members are well prepared to ensure a successful outcome.

BEING PREPARED

The reviewer and employee have specific responsibilities in a review. To ensure that the discussion is focused and controlled, understand your own role and brief employees on their responsibilities so that they, too, can prepare effectively.

22 Make the most of your review time by thinking about it in advance.

23 Plan to talk about the job – not about the person.

24 Always check that you have all the documentation you need for reviews.

DEFINING THE REVIEWER'S ROLE

The role of the reviewer is to encourage and guide the employee through the structure of the review. You should be a conduit, or a catalyst, not a judge or interrogator. Plan the logistics of the meeting at least two weeks in advance. Note the topics you wish to discuss in order of importance so that you know in advance what you need to cover. Think of questions that will encourage the employee to talk. Read any guidance notes that accompany the performance review documentation issued by your organization.

UNDERSTANDING THE EMPLOYEE'S ROLE

For the employee, the performance review meeting offers an opportunity to discuss jointly their performance, their progress, their future, their objectives and focus, and their approach to the job. To help them prepare for this discussion, issue staff with a self-assessment document and give them plenty of time to complete it. Ask them to come up with examples of high and low points, and to think about areas for improvement. Have there been any changes to their job, or aspects that have become more or less important since the last review? Encourage people to report back on projects they have worked on, or suggest worthwhile projects for the future.

HELPING EMPLOYEES ⊃ PREPARE

f-assessment questions should be efully framed to help team members pare for discussion. Ensure that staff ve ample space to be able to answer the estions as fully as possible.

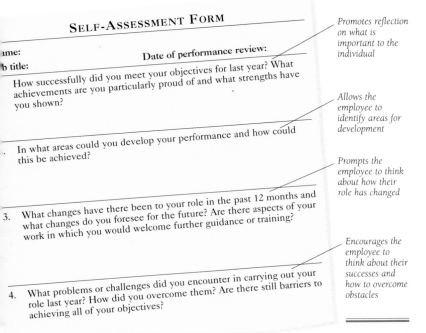

SELF-ASSESSMENT FORM

me:

Date of performance review:

b title:

How successfully did you meet your objectives for last year? What achievements are you particularly proud of and what strengths have you shown?

Promotes reflection on what is important to the individual

. In what areas could you develop your performance and how could this be achieved?

Allows the employee to identify areas for development

3. What changes have there been to your role in the past 12 months and what changes do you foresee for the future? Are there aspects of your work in which you would welcome further guidance or training?

Prompts the employee to think about how their role has changed

4. What problems or challenges did you encounter in carrying out your role last year? How did you overcome them? Are there still barriers to achieving all of your objectives?

Encourages the employee to think about their successes and how to overcome obstacles

EVALUATING PERFORMANCE

Preparing for the performance review involves looking at an overview. Evaluate an employee's progress since the last review – in terms of performance and development – to help you set new objectives and plan activities effectively for the period ahead.

25 Align the job description with the organization, not the person.

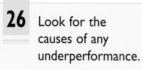

26 Look for the causes of any underperformance.

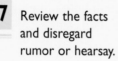

27 Review the facts and disregard rumor or hearsay.

REVIEWING JOB DESCRIPTIONS

Examine the employee's job description to ascertain whether roles or responsibilities have changed since the last review. Ensure that any alterations are in the interests of the organization, and not just the employee. If, for example, a team member dislikes cold calling on the telephone, they may have moved the emphasis of the job toward serving existing customers instead of finding new ones. Rather than allowing the change in the job description, consider training the employee in telephone or telemarketing techniques.

EVALUATING PROGRESS

Review the achievements of the employee against their specific objectives. Pick out good aspects of performance so that you can praise them, and encourage the employee to keep up their high standards. Have they approached their work positively? Have they planned, coordinated, and organized successfully? Where performance falls short of what is expected, consider the possible reasons. Ask yourself whether the area of underperformance is truly important. Negative feedback may not be necessary if an issue is minor, particularly when excellent results have been achieved in other areas.

THINGS TO DO

1. Check that the action plan agreed on at the last review was carried out.
2. If actions have not been completed, find out why.
3. Ascertain whether the employee has been rewarded and/or praised for carrying out tasks successfully.

28 Check whether staff have had the time to focus on development.

Reviewer finds out how team member has benefited from training in new software program

REVIEWING DEVELOPMENT

Having gathered information on an employee's job performance, review the benefits and effectiveness of their development activities. This is important not only to ensure continuous development, but also to confirm that the investment of time and money in developing the employee has been worthwhile. Ascertain whether the development objectives set at the last review achieved what was expected. Check that the activities improved performance to a level that affected business results. Finally, review the performance of coaches and training organizations involved to ascertain how successful they were.

◀ **CHECKING FOR QUALITY**
Follow up on courses by seeking feedback from staff on their effectiveness. Invite them to demonstrate what they have learned and consider whether the team might benefit from a similar presentation.

IDENTIFYING PROBLEMS

When planned development activities have not been carried out, investigate why. Perhaps an employee was unable to attend a course because there was a crisis in the office. If so, find out whether losing the deposit and wasting the trainer's time was truly warranted. Consider whether the employee still needs to carry out the activity. Could the need be met differently in the future? Assess whether the development activities were appropriate for the individual. For example, if after watching a video or reading a book, the information received was not applied, the employee may benefit from a different method of learning.

QUESTIONS TO ASK YOURSELF

Q Is the reason for any problem the employee may be having outside the reviewer's control?

Q What barriers restricted performance?

Q Were the objectives sufficiently clear?

Q Does the underperformance expose a development need?

Q Is the person capable of developing enough to perform as expected?

IDENTIFYING GOALS

Having evaluated performance, the next stage of preparation is to pinpoint areas for improvement and set objectives to achieve strategic business goals. Identify current levels of performance, and look for ways of developing skills and knowledge.

 29 Bring objectives in line with the goals and policy of the organization.

 **30** Prepare a list of specific objectives for yourself and your team.

FOCUSING ON TARGETS

Challenging yet achievable targets are essential if people are to feel motivated to improve performance and sustain high standards. Prepare for effective goal-setting with the employee by considering key result areas for their job. List these areas in order of importance, focus on up to six areas at the top of your list, and draw up suitable objectives for each. Phrase objectives carefully, using specific, active language, such as "sell" and "produce." Avoid vague or ambiguous terms such as "liaise" or "improve."

PREPARING MEASURABLE OBJECTIVES

Assign measures to each objective, ensuring that you will be able to access the information you need to monitor performance against those measures. Look, too, at team and organizational objectives and how these are measured. Consider the contribution that each team member must make toward this. For example, if the team's revenue target amounts to $2,000,000 and there are ten team members, you may wish to set everyone an objective of achieving $210,000. This divides the task evenly and ensures that if one person misses the target but everyone else achieves it, there is a good chance that the team will achieve its goal.

31 Be ambitious and always aim high when setting objectives.

 32 Always try to be consistent in your expectations of other people.

ETTING STANDARDS

is important to set standards, covering both the
b and personal behavior, by which competency
n be measured. To help you do this, imagine
hat ideal performance would look like. In a
stomer service environment, for example, you
ay wish to see that staff have developed an
ficient process for following up with customers
promised. Next, think how a
gh performer would typically
have – perhaps he or she would
ve the ability to listen actively
d empathetically. Avoid focusing
the people who are currently
ing the job and concentrate on
e job itself and the desired results.
ssess whether the employee is
eeting the standards so that you
n discuss development or praise
ogress in the review.

> **33** Focus on what
> would be ideal, not
> on what is being
> achieved now.

GAINING INSIGHT ▶
*Find out more about the levels of competency
needed to do a job successfully by talking to
people with experience in the role. Speak to
taff who have done the same work effectively
or refer to outside experts in the field.*

ASSESSING DEVELOPMENT NEEDS

Consider whether the requirements of a
team member's role are changing and plan
to prepare people for impending change
before it occurs. If altering roles means that
additional skills are required, assess
whether the team member has already
demonstrated those skills sufficiently, or
whether there are any areas where they are
lacking skills. If you identify a need for
development, plan which activities would
be appropriate. Prior to the review, check
that resources, such as a budget for training,
will be available for the planned activities.
Ensure, too, that you will be able to release
the team member from normal duties
during the training period.

PLANNING AHEAD

*E*ffective planning for a review involves anticipating an employee's needs and considering how best to respond to them. Be clear on what you are able to agree on, and consider timing, resources, and allocating responsibility for actions agreed upon.

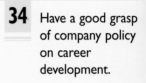

34 Have a good grasp of company policy on career development.

QUESTIONS TO ASK YOURSELF

Q Will I be able to make decisions on pay, time off, or other rewards?

Q Am I in a position to promise that someone will be promoted or trained for further career advancement?

Q Am I able to approve training and development and the budget necessary for it?

Q Do I have the authority to organize job transfers or work experience on various different projects or sites?

Q Will the human resources department agree that I have selected the best method of developing the individual?

DEFINING AUTHORITY

Make sure that you know what you will be able to agree to on your own authority, and what needs authorization. If you are unsure about this when you come to conduct the review you risk reducing your credibility as a manager by raising an employee's expectations and then dashing them later. You may also lose an individual's trust if you are forced to renege on a promise that cannot be resourced.

Manager rereads her organization's performance review policy to check that she has not missed anything

BEING THOROUGH ▶
Familiarize yourself with company policies on matters such as vacation, pay, and expense allowances so that you will be in a position to answer questions on these issues. Be clear, too, on your organization's and team's goals to ensure that any objectives agreed on will be in alignment.

35 Promise only things you can genuinely deliver.

36 Identify problems that may prevent an employee from achieving objectives.

PLANNING TIME AND RESOURCES

Estimate the duration, and start and finishing times, of the tasks necessary to achieve the objectives you have prepared for the employee. This will help you to ensure that what the staff member suggests is realistically attainable. Estimate how much time is needed for development activities and assess whether you will need cover while the person is away. Plan the resources needed both to achieve objectives and undertake development activities. Consider equipment, materials, and facilities such as working space. This well-prepared "project" plan will provide a starting point for your performance review.

LLOCATING TASKS

nsider in advance who will be responsible for rying out proposed actions after the meeting. For mple, who will monitor that milestones are met the way to achieving the objectives? Consider w exceptions or shortfalls could be reported. is task may be taken on by the employee mselves, or you might take responsibility urself, or ask a third party. After the ployee, who should be responsible for earching and organizing development rk, such as training? Finally, bear in nd that if the employee is going to take nership of the objectives, achieving m must be within their direct control.

37 Check that people have the time to lend their support.

Manager asks senior team member to act as a mentor to junior member

ORGANIZING SUPPORT ▶

If there are members of staff who may be able to assist the employee in achieving their performance or development objectives, approach them before the review to enlist their support. During the review you can then let the employee know what level of assistance they can expect.

CREATING A POSITIVE ENVIRONMENT

A conducive review environment encourages openness, receptiveness, and discussion. Build your credibility, create an atmosphere of trust, and pay attention to the layout of the meeting room to help the staff member relax and feel comfortable.

 38 Show respect for issues discussed in confidence with the employee.

 **39** Avoid telling an individual one thing and saying something else to another.

MAINTAINING CONFIDENTIALITY

To create an atmosphere in which both reviewer and staff member can talk freely, it is important to stress that complete confidentiality is expected on both sides. Prior to the performance review, make sure that you let the employee know which aspects of the discussion will be kept between the two parties, and what needs to be passed on to others, for example the Human Resources department. Having agreed to keep certain matters confidential, keep to your word and do not discuss them with anyone else.

BUILDING TRUST

Trust grows over time, and the stronger the relationship between manager and staff member, the more effective reviews will become. Earn your team's trust by putting into action decisions made during the review. The reputation of a performance review system can be ruined if what is said in the review room turns out to be a series of good intentions that are never followed through. You will need to be assertive as a manager, but you should always be seen as honest, consistent, and fair.

POINTS TO REMEMBER

● Trust can take a long time to build, yet it can be destroyed within seconds.

● If an employee suspects that confidentiality might be broken, significant items may be held back.

● Taking a few moments before the review to imagine yourself in the other person's shoes will help you to be on their wavelength.

SETTING UP THE ROOM

Create a relaxed atmosphere by choosing a suitable room and arranging office furniture so that there are no barriers between yourself and the employee. Make sure that the room is private so that you are not overheard, and that it does not have glass doors or panels – you do not want to be distracted by people walking past and looking into the room. Careful preparation of the meeting room shows the staff member that you are genuinely interested in their achievements and development. Conversely, an unprofessional atmosphere will make them feel isolated and unimportant. Check that lights will not be shining in the other person's eyes or silhouetting you against the window so that they cannot see and read your expressions.

40 Plan to start the review as you mean to continue – in a positive tone.

▼ ARRANGING THE DETAILS

When planning seating arrangements, aim to create the most informal, comfortable atmosphere possible. Using the corner of a desk is friendly, informal, and practical. It is easy to maintain good eye contact and is far less confrontational than sitting opposite one another.

Work at the same level by sitting on chairs that are of a similar size

Clear the work surface so that paperwork does not form a barrier between you

BEING OBJECTIVE

A *manager's personal approach to a performance review is critical to its success. Prepare yourself for the discussion by considering how you will encourage ideas, avoid bias, and focus on the important aspects of the job.*

 41 Carry out an objective review – not a subjective one.

ENCOURAGING IDEAS

Remember that you are aiming to encourage people to come up with their own ideas and opinions. You will learn little about your team members, or their ideas, by simply telling them what to do. Frame questions that will prompt employees to voice their ideas and take ownership of what is agreed upon. For example, you could ask what difficulties they have faced and how they might overcome them next time. Your staff are likely to be far more knowledgeable about their jobs than you are. You also want to hear their opinions, not simply a reflection of your views.

AVOIDING BIAS

One of the key attributes of a good reviewer is the ability to stand back and think about an issue before making a decision. This is especially important when conducting performance reviews, since it is vital to avoid jumping to conclusions based on superficial information. Many people tend to form opinions of others based on their past experiences of them, or may assume that an individual who shares one attribute with another person also has other qualities in common with them. There are a number of well-known types of bias that a good reviewer should learn to recognize to ensure that they are in the best position to avoid them.

RECOGNIZING TYPES OF BIAS

TYPE OF BIAS	RECOGNIZING THE SIGNS
HALO/HORNS	A tendency to allow one or two favorable or unfavorable personal attributes to color your judgment, such as assuming that an attractive and articulate individual is also intelligent.
PREJUDICE	The judgment of a reviewer is clouded by personal views of a particular group or type of people, or the fact that they resemble or remind you of an acquaintance.
"SIMILAR TO ME"	A tendency to like people we see as being similar to ourselves and therefore to recruit, and even promote, in our own likeness. This leads to unbalanced teams, where all members have the same strengths.
DISTORTED PERSONALITY THEORY	The inclination to base an evaluation of employees on distorted personality traits, such as assuming that someone needs to be an extrovert in order to be a good salesperson.
GOOD WORKER	The propensity to have a mental image of a good worker, and to favor only those who match that image. This can result in unfair criticism of employees who fail to fit the stereotype.

42 Aim to ask a team member to express what success would look or feel like to them.

BEING RESULTS ORIENTED

Make sure that the review will be focused on what is important. If you discuss side issues at length, you risk misdirecting a team member's productivity by leading them to think that these are important. You should also avoid subjective or judgmental comments. Having set targets and standards for what is important, allow employees to express results in a way that makes sense to them. An employee's success criteria can be just as valid and motivating for them as quantitative criteria. Nevertheless, it is vital for you both to agree on what is to be measured, so that there are clear indicators of what has been achieved.

PLANNING THE STRUCTURE

A good performance review is well structured. Establish the order of proceedings, and plan to get the meeting off to a positive start. Then consider how to focus the employee on key areas for discussion and deliver feedback effectively.

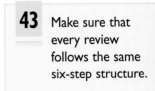

43 Make sure that every review follows the same six-step structure.

STARTING POSITIVELY

Always aim to begin every performance review with a strong motivational statement and an easy question to ease the staff member into the session and help them to relax. Next, you should agree on the purpose of the meeting, and outline what will be covered. Plan to say that you will review progress on each objective, one at a time. Aim to give the employee the chance to comment first, with questions such as, "How do you think your performance went in this area?" You will have the facts in front of you, both in terms of what has been achieved and of the feedback you are expecting to give. However, by allowing the employee to speak first, you encourage the process of self-assessment, and in identifying where you have different perceptions, you can explore the reasons why.

FOLLOWING THE SIX-STEP PERFORMANCE REVIEW STRUCTURE

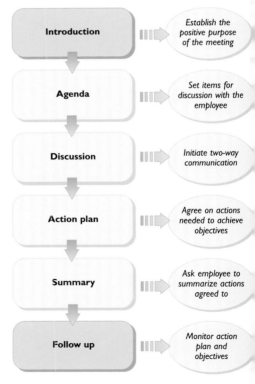

Introduction — Establish the positive purpose of the meeting

Agenda — Set items for discussion with the employee

Discussion — Initiate two-way communication

Action plan — Agree on actions needed to achieve objectives

Summary — Ask employee to summarize actions agreed to

Follow up — Monitor action plan and objectives

SETTING THE AGENDA

There is a limit to the number of issues you can effectively tackle during the review, so plan to focus the staff member on key areas so that you can agree a measurable number of objectives, say six. You may have other items to review, such as special projects, and the employee is likely to have their own items for discussion. It is important to remember that the review is not the time to catch up on operational matters. You will be holding the discussion not as part of your day-to-day management of the team, but to review the individual's overall performance and skills, set new objectives for the period ahead, and agree on a development plan. Any other business, such as a disciplinary matter, is outside the scope of the meeting and should be left out.

44 Try to cut your planned agenda in half to see if that improves the focus.

45 Focus on matters that have a direct impact on performance.

BEING CONSTRUCTIVE

If you have to give negative feedback, do so constructively, encouraging people to look forward, not backward. Avoid demotivating a potentially good employee by sounding overcritical. If performance has suffered, look first at your own leadership. Have you misjudged their level of skill or failed to provide support? If there are no external reasons, then the employee needs to understand the impact of the problem. Plan how to tackle the issues constructively. How will you get them to acknowledge that a problem exists? Think of questions that will prompt them to find solutions. He or she will be more committed to resolving matters if the idea is their own.

MAINTAINING A POSITIVE TONE ▼
Aim to "sandwich" critical remarks between positive points of praise so that you keep the ratio of two expressions of praise to one expression of criticism.

Praise → **Criticize** → **Praise**

MANAGING THE REVIEW

Managing the review involves careful choreography of the discussion. Become an effective reviewer by following a set format while remaining flexible at all times.

INTRODUCING THE SESSION

The start of a meeting sets the tone for what is to come. Launch the interview successfully by putting the employee at ease. Build their confidence, agree on what will be discussed, and explain how the meeting will be conducted to give them time to relax.

46 Make sure that the employee knows exactly what to expect.

47 Put the team member at ease as quickly as possible.

48 Stress that the review will have a positive result.

BUILDING CONFIDENCE

Many people feel nervous and apprehensive at the start of their performance review. Help them to overcome their anxieties by creating a welcoming, encouraging atmosphere. Address any uncertainties by stressing the positive purpose of the meeting and informing them how long you expect it to last. To build trust and confidence, begin with a motivational statement that conveys faith in their ability. Then ask an easy question to start them talking. Do not launch abruptly into the session by asking a challenging question early on, since this will cause them to feel defensive.

49 Check that you both set off in the same direction.

USING A PERFORMANCE REVIEW DOCUMENT ▼
Ask the employee to fill in a performance review document as you progress through the meeting. This will save the time and effort of transcribing notes later. If it has been decided that you should fill in the form, show them what you have written and gain their assent on every category.

AGREEING ON PURPOSE

Establish the purpose of the performance review to clarify why you are both there. Set out what you need to achieve from the review, focusing on the advantages to the employee, so that staff truly believe that the review will ultimately benefit them. Explain that you will be agreeing on an agenda first, reviewing the previous period, discussing progress on objectives and how development needs were met, and pinpointing any further needs that have arisen. Establish that you will be agreeing on objectives for the period ahead and then identifying any development needs linked to new objectives or responsibilities.

Purpose of job should be clearly defined in a brief summary

PERFORMANCE REVIEW DOCUMENT

Overall purpose of job:
To plan and design engineering projects to meet client specification within budget/time estimates.

Key areas of responsibility	Objectives	Deadline	Review comments on outcome
. To manage the X Port development project.	1. To keep in touch with clients at established frequency and chair steering meetings.	Jan – Feb	
	2. To submit proposal by Feb 12 and obtain project by end of March.	March 31	
	3. To source project support to within 90% of requirements.		
. To develop communications within design team.	1. To hold monthly meetings to review projects and communicate results within one week.	Review in April	
	2. Evaluate clarity of drawings and communicate results to staff twice a week or as required.	By June	

Responsibilities will be broadly summarized

Objectives should be described in a brief but specific statement

Dates for progress review meeting need to be recorded

AGREEING ON THE AGENDA

For a performance review to run smoothly, both parties must agree on the items to be discussed. Alter your agenda to include some of the employee's ideas, explain how you will agree on future objectives, and check that you have included all the important issues.

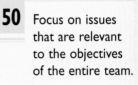

50 Focus on issues that are relevant to the objectives of the entire team.

51 Avoid being sidetracked by excessive or minor detail.

SEEKING INPUT

To ensure that the employee feels involved in the discussion you are about to have, ask them to add their own points to the agenda. Compare the importance of your agenda items with the topics that they wish to cover, and be prepared to change your agenda to accommodate them. Even if you regard their issues as less important, you must tackle some of them. If you ignore their concerns, they will feel that you are uninterested in their problems. By agreeing to include their points at this stage, you will also avoid problems later. An employee who has an axe to grind is likely to continue to attempt to bring the subject up, distracting you from your agenda. Be fair. If they are right, change the agenda.

Reviewer indicates agreed to timing and suggests deferring some less important agenda items

◀ DISCUSSING TIME CONSTRAINTS

It is unlikely that there will be time to discuss all the items on the table. Make sure that you agree at the outset which items will be included on the agenda, and which points will not be covered, so that you can arrange a meeting to handle outstanding matters at a later date.

DEVELOPING OBJECTIVES

The goal of the review is to develop a set of objectives that the employee is committed to achieving. Agree with the employee that you will discuss each previous objective in turn to identify what went well, what did not go so well, and what the employee can do about it. This may simply be to continue to maintain high standards, or to develop their skills in order to improve their performance. Establish that you will be setting future objectives in the form of a jointly agreed action plan, with criteria to measure success. You will also agree on the importance of objectives to the team, to the organization and, most importantly, to the employee if they are successful.

52 See that the employee participates fully in creating the agenda so that they feel included and involved.

ASSESSING THE AGENDA

Check that the agenda focuses on the employee's performance as it stands now. Do not assume, for example, that he or she will see the link between success in a past project and using the same skills in a new and different future project. Do not duck issues – you risk setting objectives that the employee will accept with no hope of achieving. Ensure that the agenda includes finding out what the employee believes is achievable. They may feel they can achieve more than you thought possible. You will discuss this and identify why your views differ. You may find that you think more is achievable than they do, and will need to plan support and confidence-building activities.

ORDERING ITEMS FOR DISCUSSION

Review previous objectives

Praise achievements

Give constructive feedback

Identify development needs

Praise additional achievements

Agree on new objectives

Agree on further development needs

Plan and agree on actions

Summarize

ENCOURAGING DISCUSSION

In a successful performance review, the employee should be doing most of the talking. Encourage staff to take a leading role in the discussion by adopting good questioning techniques, then listening actively to the answers.

53 Keep asking questions to gain the staff member's involvement.

54 Avoid interrupting once an employee has started talking.

55 Consider how to turn your closed questions into open-ended ones.

ASKING QUESTIONS

Good questioning techniques are essential if you are to discover an appraisee's true opinions. When you understand how an individual feels, you can use this knowledge to help them improve their performance. By asking the right questions you encourage an appraisee to bring issues into the open, rather than harbor a problem so that it festers and hinders performance. Use questioning in a genuine attempt to find out how the appraisee feels about all aspects of their job. Listen to their answers. Avoid cross-examining the appraisee or asking leading questions in a bid to confirm a preconceived notion in your own mind.

LEADING QUESTIONS

An open-ended question encourages an expansive answer, as opposed to a closed question, which typically prompts a one-word "yes" or "no" response. Frame open-ended questions by starting with the words, "What," "When," "How," "Which," "Who," or "Why." If you ask open-ended questions, such as, "What were the main learning points?" an employee is more likely to express their ideas than if you ask a closed question, such as "Did you achieve this objective?" Look at the objectives you will be reviewing and think of an open-ended question to start the discussion on each one.

56 If an employee looks confused, ensure you are not using jargon that they do not understand.

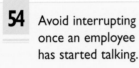

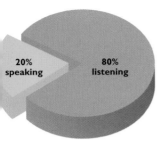

LISTENING PROPERLY
Ideally, you should aim to spend about 80 percent of the performance review listening, and only 20 percent of the time speaking.

20%
speaking

80%
listening

SHOWING INTEREST
The reviewer in this example is an active listener; his body language demonstrates that he is giving his undivided attention to the employee and concentrating on what is being said.

LISTENING ACTIVELY

Once you have encouraged the staff member to start talking, listen actively to their answers. If you are listening actively, you will be able to glean far more from what is being said. Look at the person and maintain good eye contact – but try to avoid staring. Bear in mind that even if you glance over their shoulder or out of the window, you will give the impression that you are not paying proper attention to what is being said. When they pause, or draw to a conclusion, help them to build on their ideas by asking further questions. Be aware of the tone of voice that they are using, and listen for subtleties of speech that may provide clues on what they truly think about their performance. This will enable you to build joint solutions by asking more questions such as, "What will help you to achieve even better results?"

Good eye contact is maintained

Employee feels encouraged to talk freely

Reviewer leans forward to indicate interest

37

BEING PRACTICAL

There may be a long list of issues to discuss in a performance review, most of them with significant implications for the future. Ensure that you keep to the set timing, tackle all the important items, and prompt employees to reach realistic conclusions.

57 Aim to stick to the time allocated for the review.

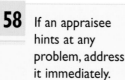

58 If an appraisee hints at any problem, address it immediately.

KEEPING TO THE POINT

Stick to the agenda and focus on essential issues by controlling the discussion so that it does not stray from the employee's previous important objectives or those for the future. It is important to complete the review in the time allocated or you risk spending longer than you can afford on reviewing the entire team, and may be forced to postpone some reviews. If a discussion on one point has overrun, consider which agenda items you can shorten, skip, or deal with at a later date.

COVERING VITAL ISSUES

If, as a result of time constraints, you are unable to discuss an important issue in sufficient depth, agree to have another conversation on the topic at a later date – and keep to that next date. Avoid using this as an excuse to postpone difficult issues; the sooner these are out in the open, the better. If there is a hint that an employee is experiencing difficulty in any part of their job, discuss it immediately. Failure to address the situation is likely to worsen it. Avoid taking action that may alleviate a problem in the short term but compound it in the future. By offering to complete the task under discussion yourself, for example, you will not equip the employee to cope if the same circumstances recur.

POINTS TO REMEMBER

● If an issue has a high impact on performance but is not urgent, it may be dealt with later.

● If an issue is urgent but has little impact on performance, it may also be left for another day.

● Issues that have a high impact on performance and are urgent must be dealt with immediately.

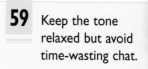

59 Keep the tone relaxed but avoid time-wasting chat.

DOS AND DON'TS

✓ Do allow people to learn from their own mistakes.

Do encourage people to think of ways of solving a problem.

✓ Do make your feedback and your agreements for the future absolutely clear.

✓ Do clarify the situation if an incorrect assumption has been made.

✗ Don't assume that you will have the best answer to a situation.

✗ Don't allow mistakes to cause people to fail in their objectives.

✗ Don't allow a staff member to leave with an unrealistic view of their ability.

✗ Don't waste time discussing skills that the employee does not really need.

60 Under-promise during a review and over-deliver afterward, rather than over-promise and regret it.

CONSIDERING IMPLICATIONS

Bear in mind that what you say to a staff member may have repercussions beyond the hour or so you spend with them. It is important to avoid agreeing to any action that may have an adverse effect on the team or on the organization itself. If, for example, you agree that a staff member should attend an external training course to obtain qualifications that are not directly relevant to their job, this could create a precedent. The result of this may be that you find yourself being pressured by other members of the team to be given similar advantages.

MOVING FORWARD

At some point, both parties need to draw a line on the past and think of the future. This is particularly true if the past has been inherited and has left legacies that cannot be changed. When you come to the natural end of a discussion of the past, signal the time to move forward by talking about the action plan. Focus on future objectives and what you both think will work from now on. Talk about future milestones and deadlines that must be achieved. Ask the employee to summarize the actions you have agreed on to check that you have the same understanding of what has to be done.

FOCUSING ON THE FUTURE ▼
Encourage the team member to look to the future and motivate them by explaining how future action plans will benefit them, the team, and the organization.

Manager points out that time management course should put an end to having to work late

39

READING THE SIGNALS

Some people struggle to raise concerns in a straightforward manner. Understand the role that body language plays so that you can read a person's body posture and facial expression to gauge whether they are holding back or responding positively.

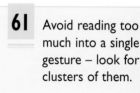

61 Avoid reading too much into a single gesture – look for clusters of them.

62 If the employee looks tense, ensure that you look relaxed yourself.

IDENTIFYING ANXIETIES

You may need to coax a staff member into speaking their mind, particularly if they are worried about what you will think, or do not know you very well. Begin with questions about easy and positive issues. Smile and maintain good eye contact. Watch for agitation and concern; this could imply that the conversation has turned toward issues they would rather hide. Listen to the content of replies and to the tone of voice used. Keep asking questions to get to the bottom of the matter, even if you are covering the same ground again.

WATCHING FACIAL EXPRESSION

When two people have a good rapport, they will look at one other throughout their conversation, turning away only to blink or think. The level of eye contact provides many clues to how the other person is feeling. If, for example, the person being reviewed avoids eye contact, there is probably a reason. Perhaps he or she does not wish to discuss the issue, is having difficulty in facing it, or is not telling the whole truth. Watch for changes in facial expression. If the person looks away at a particular point, ask questions in that area to discover what is troubling them. Avoid taking notes when they are discussing an important point, since this will interrupt eye contact and prevent you from gauging their expression.

Head held straight but relaxed shows confidence

▲ **SHOWING OPENNESS**

By maintaining direct eye contact with you, this appraisee is signaling that a good rapport has been established.

CHECKING CONFIDENCE

Watch how the person being reviewed reacts to king on each action as you proceed through the enda. Look for any signals that they are not ally comfortable with what you are asking of em. It is important that they do not have servations that will prevent them from achieving eir objective. For example, if you are asking them take on a new project or task, question them to sess their understanding of the task and their an for carrying it out. You should be able to termine their level of confidence from their tone voice and facial expressions as they answer. If e answer is "Yes," but in a hesitant fashion, this gnals an undisclosed concern, or barrier, to hieving success. Use open questions to explore s area until you achieve the response of an qualified "Yes," delivered in a firm tone of voice. ok out for phrases such as, "Yes, but …" and airly happy …," since both indicate a lack confidence. Continue the discussion until you ceive unqualified agreement.

63 Watch a person's eye movements – they can give a lot away.

CULTURAL DIFFERENCES

The Japanese tend to behave more formally than Europeans or Americans, which makes their body language more difficult to read. In the United States, body language is used to build rapport quickly, which may appear over-friendly and therefore be thought insincere by Europeans, who are more restrained.

pression ndicates disclosed feelings

Tensing of the muscles around the eyes shows contemplation

Questioning expression indicates a lack of commitment

▲ HAVING ESERVATIONS
looking downward while king, this person indicates that may have some doubts, which will need to explore.

▲ FRAMING A RESPONSE
This man is looking straight ahead but not necessarily in focus, suggesting that he is visualizing how he should respond.

▲ FEELING UNCOMFORTABLE
By her expression, this woman is signaling that she lacks commitment to doing what has been asked of her.

ADOPTING THE RIGHT POSTURE

Always maintain an open posture, keeping your hands relaxed at your sides or in your lap. By being relaxed yourself, you will encourage the other person to relax, too. Make sure that the room is neither too hot nor too cold, but is at a comfortable temperature that encourages both of you to sit comfortably. Avoid crossing your arms, since this suggests either defensiveness or that you are putting up a barrier, and avoid leaning an elbow on the desk, which could be interpreted as an aggressive gesture. Remember that you are leading the discussion, so it is important to work at looking relaxed, even if you, too, are nervous at the outset.

CULTURAL DIFFERENCES

Body language conveys varying messages in different countries. In Latin cultures, for example, touch is used as a way of establishing and maintaining rapport. In more formal cultures such as in Japan, Scandinavia, and northern Europe, this would be considered an invasion of private space. A nod in Middle Eastern countries would signal disagreement rather than assent.

64 Remember that body language speaks more than words.

65 Be aware that if someone leans back and crosses their hands, it signals reluctance.

TAKING NOTE OF POSTURE

Look at the person's posture. If he or she is perched on the edge of their seat, this suggests nervousness or anxiety. Relax them by using a friendly tone of voice, a smile, and plenty of open questions. If the employee places their elbows on the table or clenches their fists, they could be feeling suspicious or even aggressive. Keep your own body language open, but neutral, and stress to the employee how the review will benefit them.

DOS AND DON'TS

✔ Do observe what happens when you alter your body posture or expression.	✘ Don't interrupt or use a judgmental or condescending tone of voice.
✔ Do check that the person's body language matches their words.	✘ Don't look down at your notes for long periods, since this can reduce rapport.

MIRRORING BODY LANGUAGE

The study of Neuro-Linguistic Programming (NLP) provides further insights into the meaning of body language. One premise of NLP is that if two people are enjoying a good rapport, they will mirror one another's postures and use similar gestures. When one party leans forward slightly because they are interested in what is being said, the other party also tends to lean forward. When first-class rapport occurs, people may even mirror one another's breathing patterns. You can use NLP techniques to create empathy and ease tension by subtly mirroring the other person's posture. NLP practitioners also observe that people move their eyes according to what they are thinking. Thus you can gauge an individual's inner feelings by watching their eye movements.

66 Be aware of your own body posture at all times.

67 Encourage an employee with a friendly smile.

▼ **INFLUENCING POSTURE**
You can use mirroring techniques to alter the posture of an employee. By adopting a relaxed but alert posture yourself, you encourage the other person to mirror your positive body language.

Leaning forward slightly encourages the employee to participate fully

Mirrored hand positions are a sign that good rapport has developed

ASSESSING COMMITMENT

*People turn good intentions into
achievement when they are committed
to taking action. Check that staff members
take full ownership of their objectives before,
during, and after the review. If commitment
is lacking, take steps to find out why.*

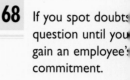

68 If you spot doubts
question until you
gain an employee's
commitment.

POINTS TO REMEMBER

- An employee who is not committed to taking action will nevertheless find ways to avoid saying a direct "No" to their reviewer's suggestions.

- The detection of a lack of commitment early on makes it easier to avoid problems later.

- Someone who feels that they have been pressured into agreement is unlikely to be truly committed.

ANTICIPATING COMMITMENT

If you know a staff member, you will be able to anticipate their level of commitment more easily Consider whether they have agreed to undertak task in the past but failed to deliver. Do they ke you up to date with progress regularly, or only when you intervene to ask for information? Thi knowledge will help you to decide how assertiv you need to be to ensure that the employee is committed to carrying out action plans. If an employee is new to your team, you should mak these judgments during the review.

OBSERVING COMMITMENT

It is important to observe the degree of enthusiasm and commitment the employee shows toward agreed objectives and performance levels throughout the review. There are a number of signs that an employee is becoming committed to the task. If, for example, they begin to elaborate on plans for achieving an objective, or start asking questions about implementation and who should be informed about the objective, these are positive signals of commitment. To test commitment, use a closed question aimed at prompting an unequivocal "Yes." If an employee is unwilling to commit, he or she will ask more questions, or voice doubts.

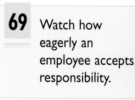

69 Watch how
eagerly an
employee accepts
responsibility.

70 Practical questions
or suggestions
indicate readiness
to commit.

ETTING REVIEW DATES

courage the employee to suggest an appropriate
e to review progress in achieving milestones. In
ing dates themselves, they take control of their
n progress and will be more committed than if
ew dates are imposed. Before agreeing on dates,
e the employee's experience into account: more
quent reviews may be needed for inexperienced
f. Make clear any exceptions to the timetable,
h as the need to be informed of any issues that
ld put a critical deadline or project at risk.

71 Stress that you will not interfere – but that you expect to be kept informed.

72 Be careful to avoid accepting a glib "Yes."

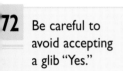

RECOGNIZING COMMITMENT ▼
*Committed employees keep their manager well informed of progress, ask
or help when needed, and discuss their tasks with colleagues. Uncommitted
mployees tend to avoid their manager and all discussion of the task at hand.*

REVIEWING COMMITMENT

A person who is committed to a task will prioritize
it. If they find that they cannot achieve a date, they
will try to negotiate extra time or suggest dropping
less urgent actions in order to complete the task.
If an employee has no intention of performing the
task, you are unlikely to find out until after the
deadline for completion. To review commitment,
consider whether the employee approaches you
with problems in good time. If you have to chase
down information, you must address why they
have not taken ownership of their task.

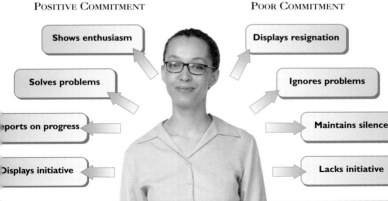

POSITIVE COMMITMENT

Shows enthusiasm

Solves problems

eports on progress

Displays initiative

POOR COMMITMENT

Displays resignation

Ignores problems

Maintains silence

Lacks initiative

HANDLING DIFFICULT SITUATIONS

A review is almost certain to cause staff to worry, since their capabilities are under discussion and their future is at stake. Be prepared to deal with the unexpected, and learn how to handle difficult situations with authority and sensitivity.

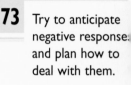

73 Try to anticipate negative response: and plan how to deal with them.

HANDLING UNEXPECTED CHALLENGES

It is important to deal with challenges when they happen if you are to retain your credibility. If an employee challenges your authority during a review, or your facts, try to deal with this at once. When you need time to think, use open questions to press the person to clarify their point. Should an employee reveal information of which you had no prior knowledge, or that sheds new light on a situation, check whether this affects the feedback you had planned.

Manager takes a long pause before calmly responding to challenge

Employee airs grievances and challenges manager's facts

Manager listens while employee speaks his mind

▲ **DEALING WITH DIFFICULT PEOPLE**
This illustration shows how, by remain: calm and framing her response with ca the reviewer was able to instigate a m productive discussion and agree action: which the employee was fully committe

RECOGNIZING YOUR LIMITATIONS

During the review, your team member may reveal information that could affect their ability to do their job. You could discover, for example, that they have a serious illness which they had kept to themselves. Maintain a balance in your goals as manager. While it is important to motivate and build relationships with individuals, you must consider the success of your team and organization. Be sympathetic, but do not start altering the existing sick leave policy at the review.

74 Recognize when to seek guidance from colleagues or professionals.

75 Endeavor to remain calm and in control at all times.

Employee recovers and the discussion is concluded successfully

When progess is reviewed, employee is successfully carrying out action plan

Manager becomes irritated and interrupts employee

Employee reacts angrily, review is stopped, and his performance begins to deteriorate

STOPPING THE REVIEW

In some circumstances, your only way forward may be to stop the review. First, do all that you can to defuse a difficult situation. If an individual is upset, allow them to recover their composure and continue when you can. Be sympathetic if tears are genuine, but be wary of tears designed to deflect you from your feedback. Try to move on and get them to focus on the next agenda item, which, if you are following the praise, criticize, praise principle, should be more positive. If the employee has stopped listening, however, there is little point in continuing. Set a date to finish the review as soon as possible.

DEALING WITH PERFORMANCE PROBLEMS

Tackling poor performance effectively is a challenge for all managers. Gain acknowledgment that a problem exists, then you can deal with it constructively by identifying causes and asking the staff member to come up with effective solutions.

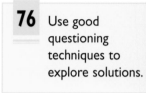

76 Use good questioning techniques to explore solutions.

77 Avoid discussing problems that do not affect performance.

SECURING AGREEMENT

Before you can correct a problem, the employee must acknowledge that a problem exists. It is important that they realize the adverse impact of their actions on meeting their objectives, or they will not commit to solving the problem. Explain how their performance has affected that of their team or the organization. Ask questions to check that the team member has now accepted that there is a problem. Make sure that they fully understand where they have gone wrong and the impact of allowing the situation to continue.

IDENTIFYING CAUSES

Having gained agreement that a performance problem exists, explore the reasons and look for ways of resolving it. Ask the employee to analyze the cause; he or she may provide valuable insight into what has gone wrong. Some problems have multiple causes. If a person is falling behind with their work, for example, there may be a need for skills training. But are there other factors to consider? Watch out for excuses or blaming other departments – make sure that the employee takes the responsibility they should.

QUESTIONS TO ASK YOURSELF

Q Could problems with organizational processes be contributing to a shortfall in performance?

Q Is the machinery being used adequate for the job?

Q Is an insufficient budget holding the individual back?

Q Are the materials being used appropriate for the job?

ADDRESSING PERFORMANCE PROBLEMS

PROBLEM	WAYS TO ADDRESS IT
CAPABILITY The inability to perform the job as defined, perhaps as a result of a selection error or lack of experience.	● Provide support and training to enable the employee to tackle the job effectively. ● If training is not the answer, consider transferring the employee to a more suitable role.
TRAINING A lack of necessary skills or information that is preventing the employee from performing to standard.	● Identify gaps in knowledge, skills, or approach, and select appropriate development activities to help the staff member meet required standards. ● Set objectives for continuous improvement.
MOTIVATION A decrease in effectiveness due to understimulation, or boredom, or stress resulting from too great a challenge.	● Identify development activities that will reenergize the employee in their role. ● Review tasks that have been delegated to the employee – are you overstretching them?
DISTRACTION An inability to concentrate and be effective at work, perhaps due to a personal problem that is claiming an individual's attention.	● Be sympathetic. If necessary, agree to time off work so that problems can be attended to. ● Recognize when to refer someone to professional help if performance fails to pick up.
ALIENATION A rejection of, and feeling of noninvolvement in, the job and organization where there is a history of long-term frustration.	● Find out how the problem has arisen: is it the result of lack of challenge or neglect? ● Consider referral to a career counselor to help the employee to resolve their issues.

78 If an employee is reluctant to take action, stress the gains to be made.

FINDING SOLUTIONS

The best solutions are those that employees discover themselves. Ask the employee to come up with a plan to resolve or avoid the problem next time. Offer your own ideas only if necessary. Discuss the options before making a decision. If their solution is unrealistic, prompt them to discuss its advantages and disadvantages, or ask them to consider the risks associated with their proposal. By asking such questions, you can help the employee to choose a more workable plan of action. Finally, agree on a short- and long-term action plan that will immediately bring performance into line, and then continuously improve on it.

DISCUSSING DEVELOPMENT

Training and development activities are aimed at helping employees to achieve their objectives and improve both short- and long-term performance. Choose activities and methods of learning to suit the employee, then agree on learning objectives.

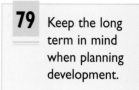

79 Keep the long term in mind when planning development.

80 See that personal development plans are dynamic and kept up to date.

DOCUMENTING DEVELOPMENT ▼
Ask the employee to record their training needs and learning objectives on their personal development plan as you discuss them. Details of the activity should be recorded by the reviewer.

DEFINING DEVELOPMENT

Training and development activities are designed to foster continuous improvement in team members' skills and capabilities in their current roles, and to develop their future potential. The help staff to welcome and learn from change, wo more effectively, and take on wider responsibilit Activities are documented in personal developme plans (PDPs), which map out current and future development goals. To agree on activities in a positive way, first talk to the employee about the strengths to show that you value their contributio Then discuss areas where development is neede

PERSONAL DEVELOPMENT PLAN

Name: NORMAN JACKSON

Development need	Activity	When	Learning objective	Results
To understand how to prioritize tasks, allocate sufficient time to each, and achieve tasks by deadline. Tools and tips to help organize myself better would be very useful	One-day time management workshop Value: $220 provided by external training provider	October	I will be able to plan my time more effectively and achieve what is important	● Learned tools and techniques to organize and plan my day more efficiently ● My performance has improved in that I can more effectively focus on important prioritie

Employee should summarize training requirements

Reviewer describes activity with details of cost, and provider

Employee should define what he hopes to gain from activity

Employee should record outcome of training activity once completed

CHOOSING A METHOD OF DEVELOPMENT

Training is often conducted on the job, with an employee being coached by their manager or a colleague, but other methods can be used to accelerate the learning process. Discuss the options with the employee to identify what is best for them. What is their preferred method of learning? Do they learn faster by doing a job themselves, or by having the job demonstrated to them? Do they enjoy reading, or would they gain more from computer-based learning? Decide on the method, when training should take place, and then plan the dates and make the necessary arrangements.

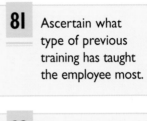

81 Ascertain what type of previous training has taught the employee most.

82 Encourage people to take up every opportunity for development.

SELECTING ACTIVITIES

The following are examples of possible development activities:

- Coaching and mentoring;
- Shadowing a colleague;
- Reading journals/books;
- Attending courses or workshops;
- Taking on delegated tasks;
- Attending project meetings;
- Being rotated in a role or transferred to a new job;
- Taking on a short-term assignment elsewhere;
- Attending conferences, briefings, or seminars;
- Gaining professional or work-related qualifications, such as first aid, health and safety, or management.

WRITING LEARNING OBJECTIVES

Just as you agree on clear business objectives with measures of success for employees, so you also need to establish what they should learn from undertaking training courses or other development activities. Defining learning objectives gives direction to training and allows you to monitor whether activities are meeting the needs of the team and its members. Consider what you want the learner to be able to do by the end of the activity, and how well you want them to be able to do it. This gives you learning objectives with two constituents – a verb and a standard. For example, if you plan to send an employee to learn more about the service you offer to customers, a learning objective might be that at the end of training, the employee will be able to answer customer questions on three of your products. Even on formal training courses that already have general learning objectives, you should still tailor objectives to describe your employee's particular needs.

DISCUSSING ASPIRATIONS AND POTENTIAL

Most people aspire to take on more senior roles and further their careers. Take the opportunity to discuss an employee's future aspirations and potential so that you can help them prepare for advancement in the future.

83 Talk about long-term prospects as well as short-term objectives.

PLANNING FOR THE FUTURE

Find out about an employee's aspirations for the future so that you can plan the support and development they need. Use open-ended questions to explore how they envision their current role changing over the next year. Then ask what the employee would like to be doing in, say, one to two years' time. Aim to identify development needs for both time frames. There are many ways of meeting development needs, such as by organizing a short-term assignment inside or outside the organization to enable an individual to gain more experience or skills.

Recognizing his potential, manager arranges training to help him further his career

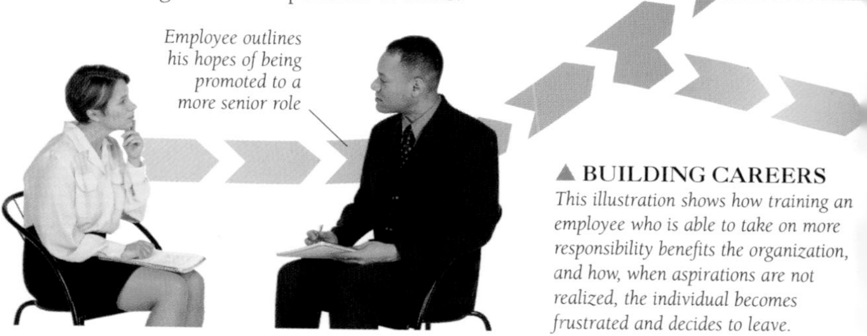

Employee outlines his hopes of being promoted to a more senior role

▲ **BUILDING CAREERS**
This illustration shows how training an employee who is able to take on more responsibility benefits the organization, and how, when aspirations are not realized, the individual becomes frustrated and decides to leave.

ANTICIPATING CAREER MOVES

Be aware of your organization's policy on career development. Look at the career paths that other people in your organization, or team, have followed. This will give you a better idea of the career moves that might be possible and enable you to answer an employee's questions on the subject. If an employee is ambitious and has the potential, a move in one or two years may involve transferring to another part of the organization. Even if you support it, do not agree to a potential move if you are not in a position to help it happen, or if it is not in line with company policy.

Employee's aspirations are realized when he is promoted to lead a new project team

Employee receives no training, becomes demotivated, and decides to find a new job

BENEFITING YOUR ORGANIZATION

It is important to keep the needs of your organization in mind throughout the performance review. Complete any career development documentation, and make sure that the human resources department and senior managers know about people in your team who have potential. Avoid trying to keep people on the team for as long as possible because you have trained and developed them: remember that new recruits inject new ideas. Remember, too, that senior management prefers "net exporters" of team members to managers who hoard their own people. Aim to become known as a manager who develops and encourages people, since this will result in more people wanting to join your team.

DOS AND DON'TS

✔ Do look for ways of promoting people who are capable of doing more.

✔ Do plan how to replace people who are promoted off your team.

✘ Don't pass poor performers onto colleagues in other departments.

✘ Don't assume that your staff will be happy to remain in their current jobs.

PLANNING ACTION

In order for an employee to achieve objectives, it is vital that they know who is responsible for which actions and the deadlines for carrying them out. Agree on and document a detailed action plan that sets out what needs to be done.

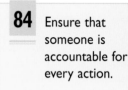

84 Ensure that someone is accountable for every action.

85 Always carry out your own commitments on time.

CREATING AN ACTION PLAN ▼

Draw up an action plan to provide a record of actions that have been agreed upon. It may be no more than a simple note of chasing down information, or it may be a more detailed rundown of new responsibilities or projects.

DOCUMENTING ACTIONS

Write down actions that arise from your discussion about objectives to ensure that you have a record of what has been agreed to. This will avoid any misunderstandings or disagreements later. Use a prepared form, or ask the employee to use a notepad. Be careful to avoid dictating an action plan, since this will not encourage the employee to commit to it. As the reviewer, you may also be responsible for a few actions, primarily those concerned with resourcing training and development, or informing people in other areas of your organization that the employee has your authority to act.

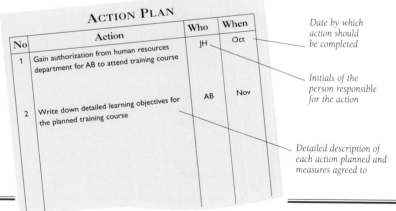

ACTION PLAN

No	Action	Who	When
1	Gain authorization from human resources department for AB to attend training course	JH	Oct
2	Write down detailed learning objectives for the planned training course	AB	Nov

Date by which action should be completed

Initials of the person responsible for the action

Detailed description of each action planned and measures agreed to

PLANNING A PROJECT

project is a series of activities designed to
hieve a specific outcome to a set budget and
nescale. Some of the objectives you agree on
ay well constitute a project. If you assign a
oject to the employee during the review, help
em to use the discipline of project management
improve their performance. Make sure that
u can measure success quantitatively and
alitatively. Finally, if you have any doubts about
e employee's ability to complete the project
ccessfully, address them. Decide how the
1ployee can overcome the skills gap, or close
with training and development.

PLANNING DEADLINES

o help the staff member use their own initiative
d take ownership of their objectives, it is
portant that you keep the actions that you agree
in an employee's action plan to a minimum.
owever, there may be issues that are beyond
eir control, such as ensuring that they are given
e authority to manage a project or work toward
objective. Let them know what you need to do,
that you can both make note of the dates by
iich actions will be completed. After
e review, allocate the time and
ources you need to enable you to
pport the employee's achievement
their objectives without doing
eir job for them.

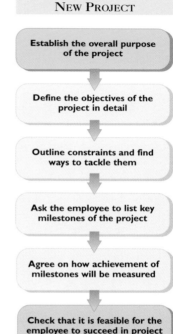

ASSIGNING A NEW PROJECT

Establish the overall purpose of the project

⬇

Define the objectives of the project in detail

⬇

Outline constraints and find ways to tackle them

⬇

Ask the employee to list key milestones of the project

⬇

Agree on how achievement of milestones will be measured

⬇

Check that it is feasible for the employee to succeed in project

Reviewer notes dates for reviewing milestones and achieving objectives

GREEING ON DATES ▶
*Make sure that there are no
iscrepancies regarding what actions
e expected to be done when, and by
whom, by writing dates in both the
reviewer's and employee's planners.*

SUMMARIZING THE REVIEW

*D*ocumenting a summary of the review *provides a vital record for both parties, and for the organization, of what has been agreed to. Agree on a detailed summary with the employee as a final check that they are committed to their action plan.*

86 Listen carefully to what an employee says, and observe how they say it.

87 Avoid dictating to an employee – allow them to use their own words.

INVOLVING THE EMPLOYEE

Using their notes, or the form that they have filled in, let the employee summarize what has been agreed to as a final check that they are committed to the action plan. If the employee finds it difficult to sum up the action plan in their own words, this indicates that they have not fully understood what needs to be done. Discuss those areas that are causing uncertainty to ensure that you both take away the same result from the review.

◀ SECURING CONFIRMATION

By failing to ask Brian to summarize an action in his own words, Helen paved the way for misunderstanding. Fortunately, the miscommunication came to light the next day, when she was able to rectify her oversight. This time, she asked Brian to state exactly what his subsequent actions would be, clarifying the situation for them both, and ensuring the prompt delivery of the stationery.

CASE STUDY

Brian's manager, Helen, had run out of time at the end of his review. As a result, she had not asked Brian to summarize the last action plan in his own words. The review over, Helen was expecting Brian to choose some stationery and order it from their usual supplier as part of a long-term contract. However, Brian thought that he had been asked to choose the stationery and then approach several suppliers for a quote. The misunderstanding came to light the following day when Brian explained to Helen that stationery could not be delivered on time. Helen asked why, and explained that it was not necessary to go out to tender. She then asked Brian to state the actions he was going to take to meet the schedule. This avoided further misunderstanding and the stationery duly arrived just before it was needed.

CLEARING UP MISUNDERSTANDINGS

If an employee omits a vital point from their summary, or misinterprets an issue, respond immediately. The employee may have altered the content, or the tone of what was said, perhaps to avoid taking action. Do not allow a misunderstanding to continue, since it will be difficult to raise the issue again without damaging the credibility and trust you have built up. If you need clarification, ask the employee to repeat the point, or give your own summary and check that you are both on the same wavelength.

88 You should both leave the review with the same understanding.

SEEKING CONFIRMATION

Aim to end the review with an agreement that is satisfactory to both of you. If there is no time to reach total agreement on important areas, arrange to discuss the issues again later. You have now completed the review form, the personal development plan, and/or the action plan. Produce copies of these for yourself, the employee, and, if required, for the human resources department.

GETTING FEEDBACK

In order to develop your own skills, immediately after the review ask the employee to give you feedback on how valuable the session has been for them. Find out how well the person thought you listened and whether the output, including action plans and personal development plans, has been worthwhile. Ask an open-ended question such as, "How useful has this review been?" Ask which parts were most useful and what could be improved upon. Giving honest feedback to a reviewer can be difficult, so observe their body language and listen to their tone of voice to ascertain whether they are being open, or keeping opinions to themselves. If you doubt their positivity, probe further until they voice any misgivings they were concealing. Ask for an additional evaluation later on (perhaps at a review session) with the question, "What results do you attribute to our last review?"

FOLLOWING UP THE REVIEW

Following up after a review is key to maintaining motivation and progress. Monitor activities and development, and evaluate the employee's and your own ability to benefit from the process.

MONITORING PROGRESS

To ensure that reviews result in the long-term benefits they set out to achieve, progress must be closely monitored. Hold the correct types of follow-up review at the appropriate time, and understand how to conduct them effectively.

89 Hold a short review, even if an employee is making good progress.

90 Ensure that you understand how people are feeling.

91 Try to anticipate problem areas for the employee.

USING FOLLOW-UP REVIEWS

Hold interim reviews to check that milestones a being achieved between formal performance reviews, to identify strengths and shortcomings, and to build confidence. Staying in touch with a employee's progress will motivate them to keep improving. Choose a type of review appropriate to the employee, according to their progress and competence level. Allow experienced staff to me deadlines on their own as far as possible, but hold more frequent reviews for newcomers, or those whose objectives are particularly stretching

Defining Types of Follow-up Review

Type of Review	When to Use It
Quick Update A spontaneous, short, and informal review with no agenda.	This is useful when people are handling a new task or role, or if something has just happened with implications for the staff member or project.
Ad-Hoc Review A 10–15 minute review with the purpose of discussing a specific topic.	This is held if the employee or reviewer are concerned that an objective may be under threat and need to plan how to tackle the problem.
Checkpoint Review A preplanned meeting to monitor milestones as agreed with the employee.	This is used to check that progress is on target, objectives are being met, and all is progressing according to plan.
Evaluation Review A formal meeting held at the end of every project to assess its effectiveness.	This provides an opportunity to find out what has been learned, to check that objectives were met, and that they were appropriate.

Carrying Out Follow-up Reviews

While it is important to build in checkpoints to ensure that the expected progress is being made, avoid interfering to deal with minor mistakes. Instead, use reviews to ensure that both you and the employee understand the nature of progress to date. Ask open questions, assess their level of confidence, and listen for unsolicited comments that might signal doubts that they can achieve what is required. If there is a problem that the individual is finding difficult to address, offer your support, but do not press them to accept it if they turn it down. Your goal is to encourage them to take ownership of the activity, think problems through, and only then offer solutions. Avoid becoming too involved in detail, since this will result in too much of your time being taken up in review meetings and cause the employee to think that you do not trust them.

Questions to Ask Employees

Q What has been achieved and what have we learned?

Q How well do you think that we have worked together?

Q Which factors have helped your progress and which have hindered it?

Q What further development needs have you identified?

Q How do you think what has happened so far might change the way in which we work together in the future?

Q Are you happy to take responsibility for carrying this improvement action forward?

Q Can you foresee any problems that could hinder your progress in the future?

IMPLEMENTING DEVELOPMENT PLANS

To help staff develop their skills and knowledge as agreed on in the review, consider which development activities are most suitable. Review development plans frequently, and help employees to monitor their progress as they implement them.

92 Promote the sharing of insights and experience in your team.

93 It is never too late for anyone to learn new skills.

PROMOTING LIFELONG LEARNING

Each team member has a unique set of skills, knowledge, and experience that shapes their attitudes and behavior. Your team members may be aware of at least some of their strengths, but the feedback that you give during reviews helps people to recognize all the skills, knowledge, and experience they have acquired. Realizing what they have learned, and continuing to learn new skills, increases confidence and promotes a willingness to use more initiative and take risks. Discuss the development plan you agreed on during the review with each individual, so that they take ownership of it and become familiar with the continual process of learning and self-development.

DEVELOPING YOURSELF ▼
Learning should be a continuous process, no matter what your age. The more skills and experiences you acquire, the more confident and knowledgeable you become.

Manager seeks to improve her understanding of financial statements

94 Encourage people to greet new challenges with enthusiasm.

IMPLEMENTING AND REVIEWING THE PLAN

Look for development activities that benefit the organization, the team, and the team member. If, for example, you know that the employee enjoys outdoor activities, such as climbing and sailing, it may be appropriate to send them on a wilderness challenge course to learn how teams form and develop. Encourage team members to refer to their personal development plans and review the results of development activities frequently. Help them to develop transferable skills that they can apply to a wide range of situations. Agree on changes to development plans that will enable the employee to react to changing circumstances and customer demands.

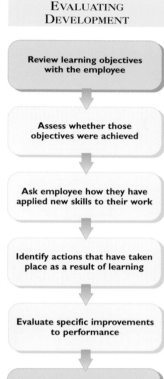

EVALUATING DEVELOPMENT

Review learning objectives with the employee

Assess whether those objectives were achieved

Ask employee how they have applied new skills to their work

Identify actions that have taken place as a result of learning

Evaluate specific improvements to performance

Record results of development on personal development plan

BUILDING TEAM SKILLS

By sending adventurous staff on courses in an environment that they will enjoy, you are helping them to learn team-building techniques that will be useful to their team and their organization. They will also improve their skills as a team member or leader in their favored leisure activities.

EVALUATING TRAINING

Hold a debriefing session immediately after training and development activities to discuss how well learning objectives were met. Debrief after every type of event, including on-the-job coaching. If there is a gap between what was expected and what was achieved, discuss how to close the gap and update the development plan with that action.

ENCOURAGING TEAMWORK

The six-step review system works just as well when used for teams as it does for individuals. Develop the skills and improve the performance of your team as a whole by holding regular team reviews and integrating training needs.

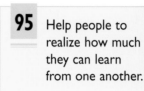

95 Help people to realize how much they can learn from one another.

96 Praise team efforts to show that you value the fact that they pull together.

USING THE SIX-STEP PLAN

The six-step plan not only provides a framework for individual performance reviews but is also useful in the team environment. Prepare the key issues for discussion, and call the team together for a combined review on how well they are working together. Explain the purpose of the session and establish what team members' roles are. If there are issues that involve one or two people and not the whole group, postpone these to a separate meeting. As you work through the agenda, ensure that people write down their actions. Finally, ask everyone to summarize their own action plans to check their understanding and commitment.

USING TEAM REVIEW ▼
Focus team members on the objectives that they are seeking to achieve as a unit. Negotiate the agenda for the meeting, and be prepared to drop items that you have outlined for discussion in favor of better suggestions from team members.

Manager concentrates on discussing items that are of interest to the whole group

Team member prepares to summarize her own action plan at the end of the meeting

Team member notes actions. for which he is responsible

97 Involve the whole team in planning its development for the future.

98 Get the most from a training budget by sharing resources.

ENCOURAGING TEAM FEEDBACK

Extend the use of the performance review process to improve teamwork skills. Ensure that the entire team is clear about their objectives and how they are linked to other teams within the organization. In addition to encouraging people to give and receive feedback during their own review, help them to be open and constructive with each other. In the open environment encouraged by an effective review, team members should be encouraged to share information and knowledge to build support and trust. Use team meetings to solve problems, build good working relationships, and review how the team is progressing against objectives.

INTEGRATING TRAINING

Group individuals with common training and development needs together so that training courses will be more economical. Keep a record for senior management of who have been attending courses, on which subjects, and the benefits. This will allow the management team to assess whether their investment in training and development is paying off in terms of business objectives. If senior managers are convinced by the business case for developing their staff, they will continue to invest. Future development plans are more likely to be approved if they build on past successes.

POINTS TO REMEMBER

- Just as consistency is needed within a single team, an organization requires consistency throughout all teams.
- Peers are often the best advisers to their colleagues.

◀ ORGANIZING GROUP TRAINING
Plan to group people with similar training needs together. This is both cost-effective and strengthens staff relations, since team members can share learning experiences.

EVALUATING YOURSELF

For the review system to work successfully, managers themselves must improve and develop skills alongside their staff. Evaluate your performance as a reviewer and ask your employees for feedback in order to become more effective.

99 Act as your own critic – but remember to be constructive.

100 Take every opportunity to learn and practice new skills.

101 Check that reviews have win-win outcomes for all involved.

MONITORING PROGRESS

To ensure that reviews have contributed to your team's continuous improvement, examine the results that each team member is achieving after the reviews have taken place. Allow a period of, say, three months to see a noticeable improvement in performance. Check that the objectives set are consistent with the standards set for all individuals on your team. To help you do this, ask staff in similar jobs on other teams to give you a benchmark for performance. Ensure that the team action plan has been implemented and that you have provided the promised support and resources. Finally, plan review sessions that are focused on performance improvement. Do the reviews demonstrate that clear progress is being made?

DEVELOPING YOUR REVIEW SKILLS

A valuable method of developing your review skills is to practice role playing. Ask a colleague who understands the employee and his or her work situation to role play how the employee might behave. If you have practiced the answer to a difficult question, you will be able to answer it more authoritatively in the real meeting. Consider attending a training course on conducting reviews. These generally tend to feature role playing quite heavily. If you do attend a training course, prepare notes on staff members you will have to review so that you will be able to use them as examples without breaching confidentiality.

EVALUATING THE LONG TERM

Study the entire performance review process and all the reviews you have conducted over the period of the past year. Reflect on what you have learned about yourself as an reviewer and how reviews have helped you to achieve results. Only when you are slightly removed from the event will you be able to see patterns clearly and identify your development needs as a reviewer. Perhaps you need further training to be able to give feedback that is motivational, even when its content makes difficult listening for the team member. Perhaps you need to clarify roles or make objectives more measurable. Look at your timetable for reviews and assess whether you allowed sufficient time for preparation, the reviews themselves, and follow-up afterward. Do you need to start earlier next time? How fair were the performance reviews, and were they consistent for all individuals on your team? What have you learned about performance reviews over the year and, for that matter, about yourself?

▼ **SEEKING FEEDBACK**
To develop your skills as a reviewer, ask team members to give you honest feedback on your performance and the usefulness of their performance reviews. Find out whether they were happy with the feedback they received, and if there are any aspects of the review process that they feel could be improved.

Manager seeks feedback on the time allowed for staff to prepare for reviews

ASSESSING YOUR REVIEW SKILLS

*E*valuate your ability to develop people through feedback and performance reviews by answering the following questions as honestly as you can. If your answer is "Never," mark option 1; if it is "Always," mark option 4, and so on. Add your scores together, and refer to the analysis to see how you scored. Use the answers to identify the areas that need improving.

OPTIONS
1 Never
2 Occasionally
3 Frequently
4 Always

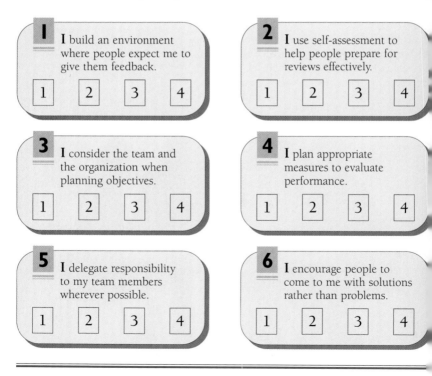

1 I build an environment where people expect me to give them feedback.

| 1 | 2 | 3 | 4 |

2 I use self-assessment to help people prepare for reviews effectively.

| 1 | 2 | 3 | 4 |

3 I consider the team and the organization when planning objectives.

| 1 | 2 | 3 | 4 |

4 I plan appropriate measures to evaluate performance.

| 1 | 2 | 3 | 4 |

5 I delegate responsibility to my team members wherever possible.

| 1 | 2 | 3 | 4 |

6 I encourage people to come to me with solutions rather than problems.

| 1 | 2 | 3 | 4 |

7 I carefully consider which topics should be raised during a review.

1 2 3 4

8 I prepare notes on the employee's past performance prior to their review.

1 2 3 4

9 I identify ways of developing people when I prepare for their review.

1 2 3 4

10 I am aware of what I can agree on my own authority in a review.

1 2 3 4

11 I conduct appraisals in an atmosphere of trust and confidentiality.

1 2 3 4

12 I treat all staff equally and am fair and objective with every individual.

1 2 3 4

13 I plan how to deliver feedback constructively.

1 2 3 4

14 I explain the format that the meeting will take at the start of the review.

1 2 3 4

15 I establish the agenda at the beginning of the review.

1 2 3 4

16 I listen far more than I speak during a review.

1 2 3 4

17 I understand that what I say to an individual may have implications for others.

| 1 | 2 | 3 | 4 |

18 I am able to discover what is at the heart of people's anxieties.

| 1 | 2 | 3 | 4 |

19 I use my body language to help the other person to relax.

| 1 | 2 | 3 | 4 |

20 I ensure that employees are committed to carrying out their action plans.

| 1 | 2 | 3 | 4 |

21 I anticipate challenges that may occur in reviews.

| 1 | 2 | 3 | 4 |

22 I ask staff members for ways to solve problems before offering my own ideas.

| 1 | 2 | 3 | 4 |

23 I agree on learning objectives before anyone attends a course.

| 1 | 2 | 3 | 4 |

24 I encourage people to consider wider opportunities throughout the organization.

| 1 | 2 | 3 | 4 |

25 I ensure that staff members write their own action plans.

| 1 | 2 | 3 | 4 |

26 I ask an employee to give their summary of a performance review first.

| 1 | 2 | 3 | 4 |

27 I review people's development plans on a regular basis.

1   2   3   4

28 I know which outside interests my staff enjoy.

1   2   3   4

29 I discuss the effectiveness of a training course shortly after it is held.

1   2   3   4

30 I consider whether individuals' training needs can be grouped together.

1   2   3   4

31 I use the six-step plan as the agenda for team review meetings.

1   2   3   4

32 I ask for feedback on my skills as a reviewer after each review.

1   2   3   4

ANALYSIS

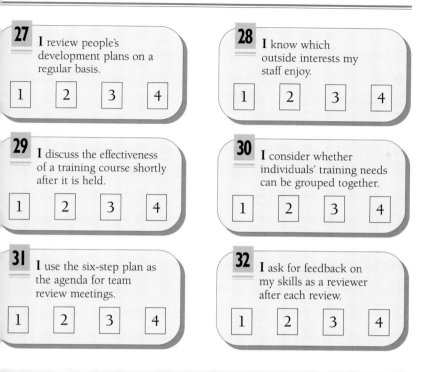

Now that you have completed the self-assessment, add up your total score and check your performance. Whatever level of skill you have achieved in conducting performance reviews, there is always room for improvement. Identify your weakest areas, then refer to the relevant sections of this book, where you will find practical advice and tips to help you refine your skills. **32–63:** Your performance review skills are not yet sufficient to succeed in getting the best from people. Check that you are preparing as thoroughly as you should. **64–95:** You are a reasonably proficient reviewer but you should identify areas for development and incorporate them into your personal development plan. **96–128:** You are a good reviewer. Avoid complacency by seeking feedback from employees.

INDEX

ACKNOWLEDGMENTS

AUTHORS' ACKNOWLEDGMENTS

A book of this nature is very much a product of teamwork, and the authors were very impressed by the highly skilled people involved in its production. Adèle Heyward, Nigel Duffield, and Jamie Hanson at DK added greatly to the content of the book, while at Cooling Brown, Arthur Brown added his design skills and Mandy Lebentz proved again a motivating and meticulous editor. Our thanks to all of them.

PUBLISHER'S ACKNOWLEDGMENTS

Dorling Kindersley would like to thank the following for their help and participation in producing this book:

Photographer Steve Gorton.

Models Roger Andre, Phil Argent, Angela Cameron, Brent Clark, Jeanie Fraser, Sander de Groot, Emma Harris, Roger Mundy, Steve Newell, Kaz Takabatake, Suki Tan, Peter Taylor, Anastasia Vengeroua, Ann Winterborn, Roberta Woodhouse.

Make-up Janice Tee.

Picture research Cheryl Dubyk-Yates.
Picture library assistance Melanie Simmonds.

Make-up Janice Tee.

Picture research Anna Grapes.
Picture library assistance Melanie Simmonds.

Editorial Alison Bolus, Fiona Wild, Kate Bresler. **Indexer** Hilary Bird.

PICTURE CREDITS

Digital Vision: 23, **PhotoDisc:** 61, **The Stock Market:** Jose L. Palaez 4-5; Jeff Zaruba 63.

AUTHORS' BIOGRAPHIES

Ken Langdon has a background in sales and marketing management in the computer industry. As an independent consultant he has advised many managers on the coaching, mentoring, and appraising of their staff. He has also lectured on strategic thinking and planning in the USA, Europe, and Australasia and has provided strategic guidance for many companies, including computer major Hewlett Packard.

Christina Osborne is a former director of personnel, an approved assessor and adviser in Investors in People, and has a wide experience in appraisals, coaching, and feedback. As chief executive of Business Solutions, a human resources consultancy, she has worked for ten years on integrating appraisals systems with the HR and business strategies of organizations in both the public and private sectors. She has sat on industrial tribunals, has lectured in business schools, and is a Fellow of the Institute of Personnel and Development and the Institute of Directors in the UK.